AF480728

Legal Courier Goldmine

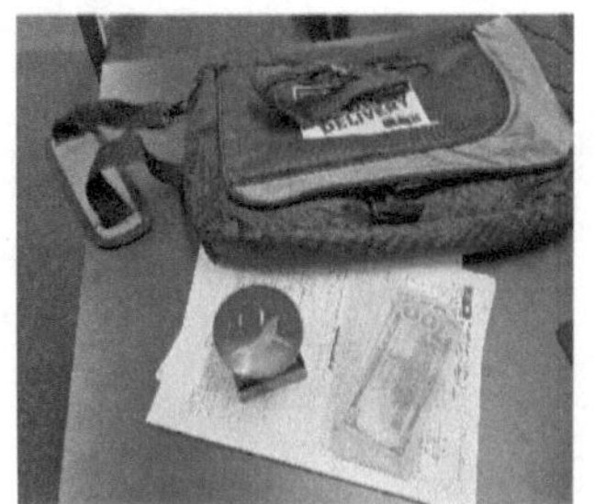

Legal Courier Goldmine

How to Deliver Packages and Process Serves to Build Your Own Hidden Empire

By Ian Hunter

Copyright © 2026 by Mindset Publishing

Published by Mindset Publishing

First Edition

ISBN: 979-8-9992885-1-6

Results and Performance Disclosure

Results vary. Building a profitable legal courier or process-service operation requires discipline, long hours, and sustained effort. High earnings are typically achieved only by experienced professionals operating established systems with support staff. Some top process servers may earn $500 per day or more, but individual results depend on execution, market conditions, and operational structure.

Legal Notice

This book does not offer legal advice or guidance on practicing law. The author is not an attorney. The material is intended to educate readers on legal courier partnerships, sales strategies, mindset development, and professional self-management within the legal services ecosystem.

A Note on This Edition

This Kindle edition of *Legal Courier Goldmine* is a focused introduction to the core ideas, frameworks, and operating principles of the business. It is designed for clarity and momentum. A more expansive edition exists separately for readers who want the complete system, deeper implementation, and long-term strategy.

Table of Contents

Dedication

This book is dedicated to the underpaid and overworked gig workers, messengers, paralegals, court runners, and process servers whose unseen work keeps the justice system alive and attorneys focused on what matters most.

<u>Introduction</u>

Your Hidden Goldmine:

Words Talk, Numbers Scream:

- ✪ There are **<u>67 million</u>** lawsuits every year in the United States.[1]

- ✪ Family Law Cases have a self-represented litigant (not an attorney) in **<u>72-90%</u>**[2] and Small Claims Cases have a self-represented litigant in **99%** of cases.[3]

- ✪ The Litigation Industry Amounts to **<u>$396 Billion every year</u>**,[4] of which Process Services alone generate **<u>>$3 Billion.</u>**[5]

- ✪ There are currently **fewer than 9,000 process servers employed in the United States** (around 8,970). This relatively small number can make it difficult for firms to find available servers.

- ✪ Many courier-servers routinely earn $300–$500/day depending on volume, routes, and workflow efficiency.

There is a Hidden Game Nobody Told You About.

Most people walk right past opportunity every single day. They drive by law offices, courthouses, and government buildings, completely unaware that inside those walls flows one of the most predictable and

---

Pew.org How Many Cases March 6 2025.
Clio.com Essential Family Law Statistics Jan 23 2026
Selfhelpsupport.org Strategic Planning Initiative July 2006
GrandViewResearch.com US Legal Services Market Analysis Report 2025- 2030.
Kentleyinsights.com Process Server Services Market Size Growth Report 2025.

profitable cash streams in America. Lawyers, paralegals, and court staff are constantly moving legal paperwork, filings, and court documents from Point A to Point B. And here's the kicker: *you don't need to be a lawyer* to make money from this system. You just need to understand how the machine works and position yourself as the person who keeps it running. This is the untapped world of **delivery, process serving, and legal courier work**, a quiet, blue-collar goldmine hiding in plain sight.

The $500-a-Day Side Hustle Nobody Talks About

While most people chase dropshipping trends or the latest crypto coin, there are individuals quietly earning $300 to $500 per day delivering legal documents and filings, often working for themselves, choosing their hours, and building real local empires. Imagine picking up certified filings in the morning, dropping off service papers before lunch, and collecting checks from law firms by the end of the day. No fancy degree. No corporate ladder. Just the right systems and relationships. And once you learn how to automate and brand your operation like the pros, your $500-a-day side hustle can evolve into a six-figure business that runs almost on autopilot.

Your results depend on your region, your effort, and your consistency. I'm not promising numbers, I'm showing what the best couriers consistently achieve and how to get there.

Why Most People Miss It

The reason this goldmine stays hidden is simple: *perception.* People assume "legal" means "off-limits." They think only attorneys and paralegals can participate. That's what keeps 99% of people locked out, and that's why those who know the truth are quietly stacking cash. You don't need a law degree; you just need a license, a car, and a plan. Lawyers are some of the busiest professionals in the world, and when you can help them save time, *they will happily pay you again and again.*

The Empire Mindset

What starts as simple deliveries can grow into something much bigger. Once you learn the systems, you can expand, adding employees, routes, affiliates you send work to and who send work back to you, office support staff, dispatchers, and even salesmen. That's when you transition from a side hustle to an *empire*. This is where the *real* money starts flowing, when you're no longer doing the work, but *owning the system.* And that's what this book is all about: teaching you to scale, automate, and dominate your region using my own previously never-shared methods.

I have always respected the men and women who keep the legal system moving, the process servers and legal courier operators who do the work nobody sees but everyone depends on. Over the years, I learned strategies, systems, and psychological tools that transformed how I approached this business, and this book exists to pass those lessons on. I once spoke with a mentor who said something that stuck with me, Before you build anything, you must know **what problem your solving**. In that moment, I realized exactly what problem I could solve if I trained the quiet professionals who show up every day, navigate chaos, meet impossible deadlines, and keep law firms alive. You are the backbone of the legal world, solving the problems of getting legal actions and cases moved through our court system fast, efficiently and correctly. This in turn ensures the rights of all to their day in court and a speedy, fair trial. This book is written to help you operate with more confidence, more clarity and far more opportunity.

Your Invitation to Play the Game

This book isn't just about making side cash, it's about shifting your mindset. You're not just a delivery driver or process server. You're a facilitator in the legal system, a business owner who turns time into leverage. Most people never realize they can step into this world without permission. You can. And once you do, you'll never look at a courthouse or legal envelope the same way again.

Legal Couriers Don't

- Need a law degree or legal background to succeed.
- Need corporate titles, big offices, or expensive equipment.
- Need permission from a firm, a judge, or anyone else.

But…

Legal Couriers *do*

- Need absolute reliability every single day.
- Need calmness under pressure when deadlines and filings stack up.
- Need the grit to drive the extra mile and handle the unexpected.

- Need to understand that trust is their currency, and consistency is how they print it.

- Need to communicate like professionals, not delivery drivers.

- Need to see every run, every filing, every serve as a chance to build a deeper relationship.

HELP WANTED:

HERMES, THE DIVINE MESSENGER –

NOW HIRING (YOUR LOCAL COURTHOUSE)

In ancient Greece, Hermes was the swift-footed messenger of the gods. He was the one trusted to deliver commands, warnings, and summons that shaped the course of history. He crossed every boundary, navigated every challenge, and carried out every mission with precision and purpose.

Today, your courthouse needs its own Hermes.

There is a growing demand for fast, reliable, sharp-minded messengers who can deliver legal documents with professionalism and integrity. These modern Hermes (known as **process servers and court runners**) are the essential force that keeps the justice system moving. Without them, cases stall, deadlines fail, and justice never reaches the people who need it.

There is a need for a Hermes to provide local services at your courthouse. Will *you* step up to the challenge and become our version of this mythological hero?

If you're ready to take on a role built on speed, trust, grit, and opportunity, a role that pays well, respects your independence, and places you at the center of the legal world, then the path is open.

Become the messenger the justice system depends on.

Become the Hermes of your county.

Chapter 1

The Recession-Proof Business Nobody Notices

There is a quiet, unsexy, highly profitable niche hiding in plain sight, that is also recession-proof. Welcome to the Legal Services Industry.

Why is this industry recession-proof? When the economy faces a downturn, there is an increase in lawsuits, legal actions and both filings and process services.

Similar to alcohol, when you are doing great, go celebrate with champagne, when you are doing really bad, drown your sorrows in a bottle. Legal work never stops. When corporations and individuals are thriving, they become a target for others to sue, and alternatively, when companies and individuals are failing, they are magnets for people suing them for not honoring their obligations, not paying vendors, breaking contracts, small claims, and bankruptcies.

Deadlines are real and in the world of court filings, process serving, and delivery these deadlines might seem boring to the outsider, but they are life and death matters to attorneys and their clients and can be lucrative to the insider.

You don't need to be a lawyer to play the legal game.

To become a certified Process Server, you do not need a college degree.

To become a delivery company owner, you do not need to go to business school or get a masters in business.

To file court documents, and serve court papers, our legal system specifically makes it open to all members of society, because we all have a right to a fair judicial system.

Process service was once the domain of sheriffs (an official duty tied to power, authority, and government paychecks) before it became a private, profit-driven profession. In the 1800s many sheriffs did not receive a salary and were paid through fees collected for their services including tax collecting, and a primary function of being a sheriff was serving subpoenas, summonses, and seized property. Towards the later half of the 1800s the cities and the country population grew and private individuals were required to track down people to appear in court. Sheriffs did not and could not handle every piece of court paperwork in large cities or the expanding west coast.[6]

We are in the middle of a historic surge in filings, deliveries, and logistical demand. Remote work has reshaped behavior, pushing more tasks into the hands of couriers rather than employees making in-person trips. At the same time, package volume has exploded, driven by the normalization of fast, bundled shipping from Amazon and other online retailers. Look at your recycling bin, if it's overflowing with cardboard, you're seeing proof of a delivery economy that has never been bigger. Someone must move this paperwork, that someone can be you.

---

[6] History of Process Serving www.shastacounty.gov. & aceprocessservice.com

Won't Email and AI replace all legal work in the near future?

Futurists have been predicting the shortening or even complete elimination of our judicial system and right to a fair trial for decades. The Process Service and Legal Courier industries have had many industry ending predictions and possible changes to the law in the past including in 1982, the proposed amendment to Rule 4 of the Federal Rules of Civil Procedure that would have permitted service by mail. Mail service is allowed today, in certain instances and jurisdictions, but it is very limited.

Email too was sure to eliminate process services and most messenger roles but that too never came to pass, although in some very specific attorney to attorney interactions, process service by email is acceptable for some jurisdictions.

Many AI predictions now assure us that the Legal Industry will be especially hit hard by the coming Artificial Intelligence Programs that will eliminate Attorneys, Paralegals, Researchers, and some are even predicting Judges and the Judicial System!

There's a counterintuitive truth at work here, often called Jevon's Paradox: when technology makes legal work faster and cheaper, it doesn't slow the system down, it accelerates it by increasing demand. The famous examples typically given are Coal, Lighting, and Vehicles. Microsoft CEO Satya Nadella invoked the paradox with AI and computing becoming cheaper, whereby businesses will be deploying more applications, using more total energy and GPU demand grows. If Lawsuits become easier to start, the general public will be more willing to sue, not less, and they will need attorneys and Legal Couriers to carry out the lawsuits.

In the movie Back to the Future Part 2, the year is 2015 and the trial takes place in less than 5 minutes. The second prediction in film came from the 2002 film Minority Report, future crime is prosecuted before a crime happens.

In reality, trials have gotten much longer, more complex, involve far more professionals, and cost more money than ever. Every year there are 67 million cases brought in the US Judicial system

This is a permanent industry with rising demand. Step in, move fast, and get paid.

Chapter 2

What is a Process Server?

My First Service *I ever completed was on a dark and stormy night. The serve was on a man who lived at an address that didn't exist, and who was not happy when I finally found him. I was given a standard legal stack of papers, the servee lived in my college town and my instructions were "go serve this." I had very little knowledge and zero experience, but I was going to get the job done. I arrived at a nearby address and drove around a mobile home park and could not find the number listed as the address to attempt service. Finally I went to the Manager's mobile home and found a directory that had a map for each mobile homes address number and location. I then got back in my car, drove to the correct house and knocked on the door.*

An old man, with a long grey beard and a beer in his hands opened the door with a mean, "Yea What do you want?" I asked are you

(Defendant's name)? "Yea so?" he said back. I then said I have papers for you and he aggressively slammed his door in my face before I could give them to him but… I had my foot in the door, so he slammed the door into my foot. Then he takes the door, opens it back up again, and slams it again into my foot. As he was preparing for foot slam number 3, I took my foot away, and he successfully closed and locked the door. So I yelled as loud as I could "YOU'VE BEEN SERVED (Defendant's first name)." And that was my first process service I ever completed. It was a little scary, very wild for me, and exciting. I made a cool $25 and knew this was just the beginning.

What is a Process Server? A process server is someone whose job is to deliver important legal documents to people involved in a court case, like handing someone a message that officially says, "You're needed in the legal process." Think of it like being the trusted messenger of the court. If the court needs to tell someone they're being sued, they need to show up to a hearing, or must respond to certain papers, the process server is the one who makes sure they get that information. That's not all though. A process server is more than someone who hands over legal papers, they are the unseen force that keeps the entire justice system moving. Courts cannot function, lawsuits cannot progress, and rights cannot be protected unless someone is willing to show up, face the chaos, navigate the unknown, and deliver with speed and precision. Without this step, the court can't move forward. Nothing happens until someone like me completes the delivery correctly.

A process server is the tip of the spear. They stand at the intersection of law, time, pressure, and human behavior. They step into neighborhoods, offices, courthouses, and unpredictable situations with professionalism and grit. It is a role built on discipline, discretion, and resilience, the exact traits that define reliable people in an unreliable world. This is why the legal community respects a great process server: because without you, nothing moves.

This is one of the rare lines of work where how hard you work, how dependable you are, and how you're known in the industry directly determine what you earn. The better you get, the more money you make. The faster you move, the more opportunities open. The more professional your presence, the more law firms trust you, and trust in this business is gold. Process servers can make hundreds per day, sometimes thousands, because they operate in a space with low competition, high demand, and skills that cannot be automated or outsourced.

This is a career that rewards hustle, intelligence, and systems thinking. You are not "just" delivering papers, you are running a recession-proof business, working inside one of the most powerful ecosystems in America. When you understand that, you stop seeing yourself as a messenger and start seeing yourself as a professional the justice system depends on, and one who gets paid accordingly.

Becoming a professional process server is one of the quickest ways to start making real, predictable money in the legal world, without needing a degree, a résumé, or anyone's permission. What you *do* need is precision, professionalism, and the discipline to follow a handful of key steps to get officially registered in your county. Different places have different rules, so check with your county clerk for the exact requirements… or get the expanded, step-by-step breakdown in the online version of this book at **mentalmodelsmastery.com**.

The Exact Steps of Each Process Service

Before Starting Become a Licenced Process Server.

Your Client Fills out Legal Documents and gives them to you to serve.

Step 1 Start Attempting service of papers.

Make attempts in the morning, after work, during business hours. When you make contact, ask if they are the person you are trying to serve, then tell them "you have been served". You can give them the papers and if they refuse, usually it is legal to drop them at their feet.

Step 2 After serving you create the proof of service to give to your client. Fill it out, sign it and date it.

Here is a link to the most common blank proof for California, you will need to create proofs and fill them out for your clients yourself, and as you get larger, you can hire an assistant to complete this step, invoicing, and other office assisting tasks.

https://courts.ca.gov/sites/default/files/courts/default/2024-11/pos040.pdf

Step 3 The client either files the proof or pays you to file with the county court clerk.

Step 1

Your customer fills out, signs and scans

Their Legal Documents

Upload in Our Portal or Submit Via Email

Step 2

You take over, review their documents. Send out for Service/Filing

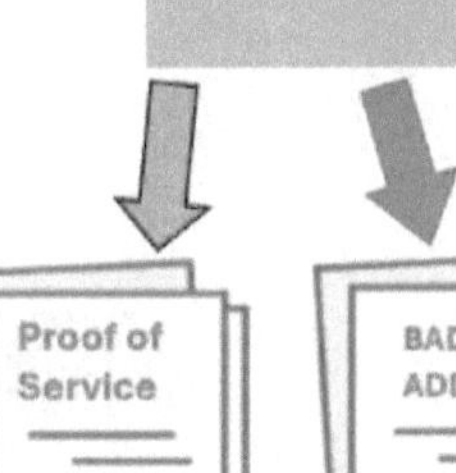

Proof of Service   **Bad Address Report**   **Filed Documents**   **Rejection Details**

Step 3

File your Proof / Reattempt Filing   or   **Serve on New Address /**

Serve your filed documents

Chapter 3

How Do I Get My First Clients?

Every day, in every county courthouse in the country, there are people stepping into the legal system for the first time. They're navigating small claims, traffic matters, criminal cases, records requests, and filings they don't understand and don't have time to learn. At the same time, attorneys are inside those same buildings, overworked, deadline-driven, and willing to pay for reliable help to move cases forward faster. Together, they represent a steady stream of customers inside your local courthouse, actively looking for someone who knows the system and can get things done.

After getting your Process Server's License, go to your county courthouse and start handing out business cards. Post on community boards and groups, both physical boards and online boards about your service offerings and availability.

You don't need anything complicated: clear job descriptions, consistent pricing, fast turnaround, and invoices sent out the week after the job is completed. Start out by offering Messenger Service, Process Serving, and Court Research. With the right software, invoicing becomes automatic, every job logged, billed, and paid without hassle. Law firms aren't impressed by flash. They reward reliability, clarity, and speed.

Here are the **Levels of Legal Courier Work** in order of experience and licensing:

1. Start as a messenger and deliver packages.
2. Offer court research and department drop offs.
3. Expand to court filing preparation
4. Then get licensed to serve process and offer all of the above.

Additional offerings could include:

- Stake outs,
- Skip tracing,
- Mail search,
- Social media search,
- Legal Document preparer
- Mobile copy services,
- Court filing fee advancement

You can learn these jobs on the job, but you must learn how to handle filings properly, knowing where documents go, which windows to use, how to confirm acceptance, and how to get file-stamped copies without mistakes. Every clean filing builds trust. Every error burns it. This is also how you begin building real relationships with law firms: show up when you say you will, communicate clearly, follow instructions exactly, and make their work easier, not harder.

Pricing: Price your jobs at increments that pay you for your time and are not too costly for your customers. Start at $50 for Court Research, $75 for Messenger Service for the first 10 miles, then $3.00 per mile after that. For Process Services, keep in mind you may have to make 4 attempts at 4 separate times and create a proof of service so add an additional $25 and price Process serving at $100.00 to start.

Appearance: Dress professionally, communicate clearly, invoice conveniently, and behave like a trusted extension of the firm from day one. The fastest way to grow in this business is to look established before you actually are.

Chapter 4

The Two Clients That Pay Forever

The Man in the Pea Coat *at my door kept knocking very loud. He was dressed very professionally and looked like a businessman. This must be important so I asked him on the ring camera, who is it? He replied I have something important I have to talk to you about. I opened the door…*

Only I was the man in the pea coat. 60 minutes earlier I was at my office and my dispatcher was complaining about a difficult serve. The guy was avoiding service, had spotted 2 different servers and kept not answering. She asked me, since you are dressed so sharp today, can you try? I bet he answers the door just because of how you look. So I headed out with the service and sure enough he answered the door and I served the papers on my first attempt.

Most new rookies take on bulk work from the large franchises at very low prices or chase new customers every week and burn out fast. But in the legal courier business, you do not need thousands of clients. You only need a few of the right ones. These are the clients who never stop needing you. They pay you over and over because their business never stops moving paperwork. Filings, service packets, discovery documents, and certified mail all have to move every single day. When you become the trusted person who keeps their operation running, you become part of their system. That is why I call them

<u>The Two Clients That Pay Forever</u>.

Client One: The Attorney, The Rainmaker Relationship

Lawyers are your foundation. Every law firm, no matter the specialty, needs a reliable way to move documents fast. Their time is money, and when you save them time, you make yourself valuable. You are not just a delivery driver. You are a silent partner who keeps their cases alive and their clients happy. Once a lawyer trusts you, they will give you work without even asking for quotes.

Client Two: The Affiliate, The Secret Referral Network

Affiliates are your multipliers. They are paralegals, investigators, mobile notaries, or other couriers who already have more work than they can handle. They are happy to send overflow jobs your way if you are dependable. Building a network of affiliates can double your income without spending a dollar on advertising. You become the person who makes their life easier, and in return, you get a steady stream of work. In Chapter 7, The Social Media Expansion Map, I show you in detail how to build your own network of referrers who send clients to you on autopilot while you focus on service and growth.

Your Forever Client Formula

These two clients are the key to building predictable income that lasts for years. Attorneys and insurance companies never stop needing your services. You do not need to be everywhere. You only need to be valuable to the right people. When you focus on serving them with consistency, speed, and professionalism, you create a business that pays you again and again.

Legal Courier Goldmine By Ian Hunter

Chapter 5

Trust Comes From Experience,

Not Theory.

I am driving on the freeway, approaching one of the many bridges in the area. I radio another messenger, I have to get those documents you have in your car. Dispatch is telling me you grabbed my stack. Pull over and I will take them from you. He radio's me back, roll down your window.

On the freeway...

driving 60+mph...

he pulls up beside my car...

I roll down my passenger side window..

He throws the documents into my lap...

He was a wild driver and a wild guy, and one of the many characters I met working in this industry, and he was a fast messenger but in this instance we could have completely lost the client's documents.

This book is not theory.

It's not written by a consultant who studied the industry from a distance. It's written by someone who has lived inside it, under deadlines, inside court hallways, on phones with impatient attorneys, and in the middle of operational chaos.

Over years in this industry, I've had more arguments with attorneys than I care to remember, and they are paid to argue. I have always thought if you are aggressive and like verbal fights, become an attorney. I have seen what really happens behind the scenes: the pressure attorneys don't talk about, the mistakes couriers make that quietly cost clients cases, the last-minute saves that never show up in official records, and the operational breakdowns that separate amateurs from professionals.

I've worked through tight deadlines where minutes mattered. Courts close and they will not wait for you, they lock you out. I have been to some courts that closed unexpectedly for the day, or the power goes out and you and your client miss the deadline.

I've navigated courthouse chaos when lines stretched, clerks were overwhelmed, and filings had to be accepted minutes, even seconds before time ran out. I've made last-second recoveries on jobs that looked impossible hours earlier. I've watched strong client relationships save businesses, and watched poor judgment quietly destroy them. I learned that energy flows, sometimes from a mad client, to their attorney getting mad, then taking it out on their paralegal, to the paralegal needing someone to blame and as the saying goes "don't blame the messenger" they still blame the messenger and save face.

I have had attorneys make mistakes, I catch the mistake, point it out, then the attorney gets angry at me!

've made mistakes myself and missed deadlines.

've learned lessons the hard way.

've seen what works in the real world and what only sounds good in heory.

But this book doesn't list those moments for drama. This is not a dramatic novel, this book is your manual to get started at building your own Legal Courier Company.

Because in business, in law, and in high-pressure environments, trust doesn't come from theory.

It comes from experience.

Chapter 6

The Freedom Framework: Scaling Without Losing Your Mind

Why Most People Stay Stuck

Most small business owners build themselves a trap. They start making money, but they are chained to every delivery, every phone call, and every client emergency. They confuse being busy with being free. They know they can do a better job than anyone they hire, it is just faster if I do the job, then train someone who might make a mistake. I have seen many small business operators work 12 or even 14-16-hour days 6 days a week, because they are unable to train and delegate tasks. True freedom is when the business runs even when you are not there. The Freedom Framework is your roadmap to building a business that grows without you doing every job yourself. It is not about hiring a big team or spending money on ads. It is about building smart systems for sales, hiring, and marketing that work together and create predictable growth.

Sales in this business should multiply naturally when the right systems are in place. You are not just a salesperson, you are a problem solver. That is what clients pay for. The secret is to build sales processes that run on structure, not emotion. You do not want to depend on luck or charm. You want a repeatable system. Create simple scripts, email templates, and follow-up routines that anyone on your team can use. Teach them how to listen, how to present your service options and prices, and how to close without pressure.

Growth in this business comes from trust, not headcount. Scaling is not about hiring fast. It is about hiring right. You do not need an army. You need two or three people you can trust. Start by finding someone who treats your business like their own. Train them personally. Let them shadow you, learn your routes, and understand your standards. When you find the right person, invest in them. People stay loyal when they feel respected and appreciated.

In this industry, the work itself is the marketing. Marketing is not something you do after the work. It should be part of the job itself. Every client interaction is a chance to build credibility. Your business name, invoices, and your email signature are silent sales tools. Use a clean professional business name that sounds trustworthy and clear. Add proof to every interaction: screenshots of successful deliveries, testimonials, and timestamps that show reliability. Your invoice should look as professional as a law firm's. Your email signature should include your title, website, and a short credibility statement such as "Trusted by over 50 law firms across California." This is marketing that happens naturally while you serve clients.

Real freedom in this business comes from structure, not effort. Freedom does not come from doing more. It comes from organizing better. Document your daily routines so others can follow them. Create checklists for pickups, deliveries, invoicing, and client communication.

Once those systems are in place, you can step away and the business still runs. That is real freedom. When you master The Freedom Framework, you no longer own a job, you own a machine. In the next chapter, I will reveal The Social Expansion Map, a blueprint for turning your small operation into a regional brand that dominates your market while you enjoy the lifestyle you built it for.

The Freedom Framework

Your Business Runs Even When You Are Not There By:

    A. Repeatable Sales Process

    B. Hiring Trustworthy Employees

    C. Delegating Tasks

    D. Add Marketing To Your Job Process

Chapter 7

The Social Media Expansion Map

The Blonde bombshell in the red sportscar drove up, started making a commotion outside, so I had to go help her…

One of the greatest film makers of all time Jean Luc Goddard once said all you need to make a movie is a beautiful woman and a gun. I never even needed a gun to make a beautiful process service.

We had a very difficult process serve and the man was avoiding service. We tried early in the morning, we attempted after work, we even tried a pizza trick where the server had an empty pizza box and tried to deliver the papers inside the box. He did not bite and we could not get him served. The man's house overlooked the street but was behind a gated driveway so he could see who was outside but would never answer the door.

So one day we had our wonderful female server put on a long blonde wig, wear a little black dress with high heels and borrow the boss's red convertible sports car.

We knew the man we were trying to serve would be home at a certain time and we had our server pull up, Rev the engine and make noise *on the street below his window. She then popped the hood and played the beautiful woman in distress with a broken down car.*

The man was outside and down on the street in 5 minutes and approached her wearing his coolest pull over sweater and sunglasses and offered to not only help but also take our server out for coffee.

"You have been served." She got him served.

Most businesses do not fail because they are bad, they fail because no one notices them. Most small business owners build in silence. They do the work, make deliveries, and go home, while other companies with half their skill get all the attention. In today's world, attention is currency. You cannot just be good at what you do; people have to *see* that you are good at what you do. What follows is a method for turning your daily operations into social proof and ongoing marketing momentum. Every delivery, every client win, and every networking event can become a story that attracts new followers and paying clients. The goal is not to fake success, it is to *document* the real one you are building in real time.

The "Share As You Build" Method

The fastest way to stand out in this industry is to be visible and human. Your company should have a personality. Most legal couriers and service providers hide behind logos and business cards. That is a mistake. People buy from people they trust and recognize. Show your face. Let people see the person behind the business. Post about your wins, your challenges, and the lessons you learn on the road. Share stories of great customer service, funny courthouse moments, or how your company helped a law firm meet a tight deadline. When people feel like they know you, they start rooting for you, and once they root for you, they buy from you.

Local dominance is built face-to-face, not from behind a desk. You cannot dominate your local market if you never leave your office. Go where business happens. Join your Chamber of Commerce. Attend local bar association mixers. Visit insurance and real estate networking events. Show up with confidence, business cards, and a clear story about what you do. You are not just another courier; you are the professional who keeps the legal world moving. When you show up consistently, people begin to see your company as part of the business community itself.

Social media is not about shouting about yourself, it is about *connection*. Most business owners post endlessly about what they do but never engage with anyone else. Flip the script. Share posts from your clients and partners. Congratulate other companies publicly. Comment on updates from law firms, insurance professionals, or fellow entrepreneurs. When you amplify others, they notice, and they remember you. This creates a network of people who want to share your content too. Before long, you become the hub of a local ecosystem of professionals who see you as a genuine, trusted connector.

When visibility is intentional, growth begins to compound on its own. When you combine online sharing with real-world networking, your reputation compounds like interest in a savings account. Each post, event, and interaction becomes another brick in your brand. This is how you grow from being a service provider to a known name in your region. The "Share As You Build" Method turns your everyday grind into a marketing machine that works even when you sleep.

Chapter 8

Mental Models to Become a Successful Owner

My passion beyond even business and sales are Mental Models.

I am working on a larger, more comprehensive mental models book that I will be releasing in the near future and there are two mental models that will level you up in your journey to become a legal courier owner and success.

The first is a basic lesson on self talk.

Program Your Brain Like a Computer To Become Successful

I have sold legal services and guided attorneys towards profitable practices and what I learned early on, is that you will never be able to grow and sell without first selling your ideas and services to yourself. You have to believe in yourself or others will not buy what you are selling. Self talk is the way forward. Here is a lesson in self talk...

Before you open your mouth to a client, you are already selling. The first person you ever sell is yourself. What you say in your own mind is the foundation for every word, every pitch, and every close.

Your inner voice controls your results. If you tell yourself you are not good enough, that voice becomes your truth. If you tell yourself people do not want to hear from you, you will hesitate and never make the call.

But when you speak to yourself with power, clarity, and persistence, you create a different future.

I learned this lesson during one of the lowest points of my life. After another rejection that left me feeling crushed, I sat in my car and said out loud, "Maybe I am not cut out for this." That sentence nearly broke me. In that moment I realized I had been repeating negative phrases in my head all day without even knowing it. I was sabotaging myself before the customer ever said a word.

That night I made a decision. I would no longer let the voice in my head push me around. I wrote down three affirmations that I would repeat before every sale, no matter how I felt. The Three Affirmations to reset your mental state before a sale are:

1. **I am a successful business owner and people are lucky to work with me.**
2. **Every no brings me closer to a yes.**
3. **I create success with my words and my actions.**

The next day I walked up to the courthouse with those words running through my mind. It felt different. I had not changed my pitch. I had not learned any new techniques. But I showed up with confidence instead of fear. And the customers felt it. I closed a sale.

This is the power of self-talk. It shapes your energy, your presence, and the way people respond to you.

Self-talk is not a trick or a gimmick. It is the steering wheel of your life. When you learn to control it, you control your outcomes.

Say to yourself, repeatedly:

"I run a great legal courier company. I go out and find new business for myself. I provide a great service."

"I run a great legal courier company. I go out and find new business for myself. I provide a great service."

Chapter 9

The Big Reveal:

What You Need to Build Your Legal Empire

What you've seen so far is only the visible layer of how this business actually works. By now, you've seen the surface of this business, daily deliveries, repeat clients, and the reputation that compounds when you show up consistently.

But the real power runs deeper.

Most people believe they only need "just enough" information to get started. In legal services (especially in process serving) that mindset is exactly what keeps people capped at the bare minimum. They stay busy, but never build leverage.

The operators who rise faster, earn consistently, and last longer understand the *full picture*. They know where long-term clients actually come from. They understand which work compounds and which work drains time. And they treat this business as a system, not a hustle.

That's why a full edition of this book exists.

The expanded version goes beyond the overview you've read here. It shows where the highest-value, long-term clients really come from, and why most couriers never find them. It explains how trust is built with attorneys, how confidence is projected without force, and how simple sales conversations quietly double income without pressure or manipulation.

It also covers the practical foundation: licensing, bonding, compliance, and the specific mistakes that delay new operators by months or years. The goal is not just to get started, but to operate like a professional from day one.

Finally, the full edition introduces the mental discipline required to stay steady when pressure rises, when timelines tighten, clients demand more, and the business starts to scale. That internal stability is what separates side work from a real operation.

This lite edition was designed to give you clarity and direction.

The full edition is for those who want the complete framework.

The expanded edition is available at:

www.mentalmodelsmastery.com

Conclusion

From Legal Couriers to Professional Operator

If you've read this far, you already see it. You see the patterns behind the couriers and process servers who quietly build real businesses while others stay stuck running routes forever.

It's not luck. It's mindset, systems, and positioning.

You can outsource tasks.
You can automate workflows.
You can hire help.

But none of that matters if you never upgrade the way you think about the work. The ceiling on most legal courier businesses is not technology. It's mindset.

The moment you stop seeing yourself as "just a courier" and start seeing yourself as a professional problem-solver for law firms… that is the moment everything changes.

Every successful courier is already in sales, whether they admit it or not.

You sell filed documents.
You sell served papers.

You sell accuracy.

You sell speed when time matters.

You sell certainty when stakes are high.

You sell calm in the middle of chaos.

And most importantly, you sell trust.

Understanding how legal work actually moves was the first layer.

This book gave you that map.

It showed you how orders are created, how deadlines drive value, how firms think, and how to build a machine that produces reliable income instead of daily stress.

Now the real work begins.

Execution.

Consistency.

Doing the simple things long enough for them to compound.

Legal Courier Goldmine was never meant to be theory.
It was meant to be a field manual.

If you apply what you've read here (step by step), you will already be ahead of 90 percent of the people in this industry.

The opportunity is wide open for professionals willing to show up prepared, organized, and serious about their craft.

This book gave you the blueprint.

What you build with it is up to you.

Stay up to date with all my writings at www.mentalmodelsmastery.com

Special Section

3 Ways to Serve Process

There are three ways to serve process on (give a copy of the claim to) the defendant:

1. **Personal Service**

➢ A copy of the claim is delivered personally to the defendant by someone over the age of 18 who is not a party to the case.

➢ Private Process Servers - These agencies will provide service of process for a fee.

➢ The person who serves the defendant must complete a "proof of service" form verifying that the defendant was properly served with a copy of the claim.

2. **Certified Mail**

➢ Service by certified mail **must be done by the clerk of the court**.

➢ The clerk of the court where you filed your claim will send a copy of the claim by certified mail.

➢ There is a fee for this service.

➢ Important Note: If the named defendant does not sign the receipt for certified mail, the service of process is invalid.

3. **Substitute Service**

➢ This is a two-step process where someone other than the defendant personally receives a copy of the claim.

Step 1. The first copy must be delivered to someone over the age
of 18 at the defendant's:

a. Residence - left with a competent member of the
household
b. Place of business - left with a person apparently in
charge of the office
c. Usual place of mailing other than a U.S. Postal Service
Box

Step 2. A second copy must be mailed to the defendant at the
same place where the first copy was delivered. **The mailing
must be by regular mail, not certified mail.**

For additional rules of Process Serving, Types of Process
Services and more in depth requirements, refer to either
the expanded version of this book at
mentalmodelsmastery.com or the following resources.

Nationwide Codes of Civil Procedure:

law.cornell.edu/wex/table_civil_procedure

serve-now.com/resources/process-serving-laws

usmarshals.gov/what-we-do/service-of-process/criminal-process/methods-of-service-individuals-state

National Organizations:

Napps.org

Serve-Now

Legal Courier Goldmine By Ian Hunter

This is only one side of the legal world. In my upcoming book, *From JD to Rainmaker*, I pull back the curtain on law firms and attorneys to show why some firms scale effortlessly and why a small group of lawyers become rainmakers while others never do. *From JD to Rainmaker* begins where outcomes are decided: inside the systems, partnerships, and mental frameworks elite attorneys rely on under pressure. Chapter 1 opens that door.

Legal Courier Goldmine   By Ian Hunter

FROM JD TO RAINMAKER

REAL SALES TECHNIQUES AND TOOLS LAWYERS NEED TO BUILD A THRIVING PRACTICE

BY IAN HUNTER

The following chapter is an excerpt from the forthcoming book **From JD to Rainmaker.**

Chapter 1

Most attorneys believe law firm growth is about working harder or becoming a better lawyer.

The data proves otherwise.

- **70–90% of law firms never grow beyond a small practice**
- **67% of law firms say getting new clients is their top challenge**
- **52% of attorneys report burnout or chronic stress**
- **Less than 10% of law schools offer meaningful training in sales, marketing, or client acquisition**
- **Attorneys bill only 2.5–3 hours per day on average**

Growth is a psychological and strategic problem, not a legal one.

If you are brand new to the Legal Industry, here is some advice if you are unable to find paying customers for your budding law practice:

So you've graduated law school and passed the bar, you finally have your JD, what now? What if I can't get a job at a firm that pays well?

I have personally known multiple attorneys in this exact dillema and have even had an attorney that worked at our Legal Courier Company, the goldmine I wrote about in my previous book Legal Courier goldmine.

One option is to work for a non profit like Legal aid, or Housing Rights, or another organization of your choice that you have passion about. Work hard, get yourself and your work out their, and after a few months, not years, Job offers will start coming in. The other option is pro Bono and finding people who have a case, and offering to be their counselor for a third of the winning if you win your case, and no charges if you lose, because you believe in them and their case.

Lastly most county public defenders are way overworked and underpaid. Walk in and ask to help for free. You will learn a lot and maybe be offered a job.

What Nobody Tells You About Growth in Law

You already know how to argue cases.
You already know how to bill hours.
But there's a hidden game being played in every law office across America, and it's not about who knows the law best.

It's about who controls time, process, and perception.

The firms that grow year after year aren't just good at the law. They're good at *leverage*. They know how to multiply output without multiplying stress. And one of their quietest, most overlooked secrets is how they manage their behind-the-scenes flow- filings, deliveries, court documents, client updates.

They don't do it themselves.
They don't rely on chaos.
They partner strategically.

That's what this book is about - the "invisible side" of your firm's growth engine.
I'm going to show you how to think differently about the small things, the logistics, the speed, the professionalism that surrounds your client experience, and how those small things quietly build a *bigger* firm.

This isn't theory.
This is how top firms actually scale.

And once you see it, you can't unsee it.

By the end of this short book, you'll understand exactly how to use the right partnerships and systems to grow your practice, and why 90% of firms are missing it. You'll also see how to go one step further - how to think, act, and persuade like the people who *win business* in every industry, not just the law.

Law firms don't need bigger offices or larger staffs to grow.

Law firms don't need endless meetings, new software, or more complicated systems.

Law firms don't need to burn out paralegals or overload attorneys with errands.

But…

Law firms do need predictable operations that run even on their busiest days.

Law firms do need filings, serves, certified copies, and court runs handled with zero mistakes.

Law firms do need to protect their billable hours by removing the tasks that steal them.

Law firms do need a courier partner who provides certainty, not more chaos.

Law firms do need speed — because deadlines don't move and clerks don't wait.

Law firms do need operational clarity so attorneys can focus on advocacy, not errands.

Law firms do need a system where their staff stops running around… and starts producing real legal work.

Law firms do need to see that outsourcing is not an expense — it's leverage.

Law firms do need to understand that every minute not spent in the office is a minute not billing.